Camping

Mason Crest

THE GREAT OUTDOORS!

Camping

Discovering Nature

Fishing

Hiking and Backpacking

Horseback Riding

Hunting

Mountain Biking

Snow Sports

Survival Skills

Water Sports

Camping

JIM BRADY

Mason Crest
450 Parkway Drive, Suite D
Broomall, PA 19008
www.masoncrest.com

Printed and bound in the United States of America.

Series ISBN: 978-1-4222-3565-2
Hardback ISBN: 978-1-4222-3566-9
EBook ISBN: 978-1-4222-8311-0

First printing
1 3 5 7 9 8 6 4 2

Produced by Shoreline Publishing Group LLC
Santa Barbara, California
Editorial Director: James Buckley Jr.
Designer: Patty Kelley
Production: Sandy Gordon
www.shorelinepublishing.com

Cover photographs by Wavebreakmedia/Dreamstime.

Names: Brady, Jim, 1951-
Title: Camping / by Jim Brady.
Description: Broomall, PA : Mason Crest, 2017. | Series: The great outdoors |
   Includes webography and index.
Identifiers: LCCN 2016002434| ISBN 9781422235669 (Hardback) | ISBN
   9781422235652 (Series) | ISBN 9781422283110 (EBook)
Subjects: LCSH: Camping--Juvenile literature.
Classification: LCC GV191.7 .B73 2017 | DDC 796.54--dc23
LC record available at http://lccn.loc.gov/2016002434

CONTENTS

KEY ICONS TO LOOK FOR

Words to Understand: These words with their easy-to-understand definitions will increase the reader's understanding of the text, while building vocabulary skills.

Sidebars: This boxed material within the main text allows readers to build knowledge, gain insights, explore possibilities, and broaden their perspectives by weaving together additional information to provide realistic and holistic perspectives.

Research Projects: Readers are pointed toward areas of further inquiry connected to each chapter. Suggestions are provided for projects that encourage deeper research and analysis.

Text-Dependent Questions: These questions send the reader back to the text for more careful attention to the evidence presented here.

Series Glossary of Key Terms: This back-of-the-book glossary contains terminology used throughout this series. Words found here increase the reader's ability to read and comprehend higher-level books and articles in this field.

Educational Videos: Readers can view videos by scanning our QR codes, providing them with additional educational content to supplement the text. Examples include news coverage, moments in history, speeches, iconic sports moments and much more!

Camp Out!

A group of three kids, maybe around 15 years old, sat in their front yard on a summer's afternoon and looked at all the stuff they'd spread out in front of them. Shoes and socks, short pants and long pants, a couple of shirts each, jackets, hats and gloves were in one pile. Another pile was of food: sandwiches, steel canteens of water, a couple of oranges and apples, and cookies. Next to that was a pile of other stuff they figured they'd need: flashlights, batteries, pillows, sleeping bags, a canvas tarp, a tent, a book of scary stories, and one backpack each to put it all in.

Think that will be enough? they wondered. They tried to cram it all into their packs. Most of it fit. Forget the pillows, they thought; we'll use our packs for pillows. We don't need the tent, either. It won't rain. Now it all fit, and when early evening arrived, it was time to go on their camping trip. They quickly hugged their parents goodbye and hoisted their packs, and walked-off on their big camping adventure, which was to a park by a creek about a half-mile away.

They waved to the adults as they went around the corner, high-fived each other and let out a couple of loud hoots, and then arrived at the park about 20 minutes later, feeling excited and then kind of far away as evening settled in.

They laid out their tarp in a clearing near the creek and threw rocks in the water until it got near dark.

Hey, who gets to sleep in the middle? This tarp isn't very big. Think we have enough room on it for all three of our sleeping bags? It's getting kind of dark. I'm hungry. Where's my sandwich? Let's turn our flashlights on. Hey, cool, mine has a red light on it! It makes my sandwich look weird.

Let's get into our sleeping bags. So, I think I'll just lie here and...whoa! Did you see that shooting star? Man, I wonder if it's going to crash into the mountains or ocean.

The sky looks huge. What's that cloud? Do you think it will rain? That's not a cloud, that's just a million zillion stars. It's called the Milky Way. Why's it called that? Hmmm, I don't

Wake up! After a night in a comfortable sleeping bag, it's time to hit the trail!

know. How about you guys? I'll Google it tomorrow. Hey, you guys awake?

The next morning the boys woke up really early when the first light started to show in the eastern sky. Their sleeping bags and packs were wet from the dew, their shoulders were all dirty with leaves and sticks from where they'd rolled-off the tarp, their hair stood all off in crazy directions and they laughed when they saw each other in the morning light.

They lay in their bags and finished their sandwiches and cookies. When the sun was finally all the way up they decided it was time to go home, so they put most of the stuff in their packs, carried the wet sleeping bags in their arms, and headed back up the street. Their first-ever camping adventure by themselves was over.

Hey, that was cool! Where do we want to go camping next week? Where do we want to go when we grow up?

Camping lets you visit amazing places with world-class views.

Turns out that over the years, those kids camped farther and farther, longer and longer away from their homes as they grew up. Turns out one of 'em was me!

I've camped in the mountains near my home, I've hiked for hundreds of miles in the Sierra Nevada Mountains of California, lived and camped in Africa and Australia, even rode my bike from Canada to Mexico along the Rocky Mountains Great Divide, and camped every night on the 2,300-mile (3,710-km) adventure.

Now I'd like to share some stories and ideas that will get you out there camping!

CHAPTER 1

Into the Great Outdoors!

Why do people go camping, anyway? People camp for many different reasons and in many different ways. But no matter how you camp, there's something that feels good about returning to a simpler way of life. Less stuff. Slower pace. And, when you think about it, camping is how we humans lived for thousands of years: cooking over a fire, sleeping under the stars or in a simple shelter, telling stories and legends into the night. Going into "The Great Outdoors" is really about *returning* to the Great Outdoors.

 WORDS TO UNDERSTAND

astronomy the study of stars and space

self–sufficient able to survive on one's own without outside help

The dictionary definition of camp is interesting:

Camp:

a: a place usually away from urban areas where tents or simple buildings are erected for shelter or for temporary residence

b: a settlement newly sprung up

There's that word *simple* again.

Here are some reasons people have given as to why they camp:

- For the environment, so that families, especially children, can observe the world around them, especially the natural world. It's a way for kids and adults to truly feel a part of the world, really know it, and learn from the experience.
- For the adventure (and for the fun).
- To get closer. I have met young people who said the camping experience brought them together. They said they are even closer friends after the experience. They liked the simplicity of carrying on their backs only what they needed. They felt it was calming and centering to know they could survive, even thrive, on their own.
- To learn and practice basic outdoors skills, like fire-making, cooking, knot-tying, weather watching, even **astronomy** and navigation.
- To get to know yourself. Just about every camper agrees that camping under the stars makes us feel good!

What do you want to learn from the experience of camping? Do you want to have an adventure with your friends? To sleep outside and see the stars? To make a campfire? To cook your own food? To show that you can take care of yourself and be independent?

Some kids go to a summer camp and sleep in cabins, while some go on hikes and camp each night in different places. Others visit a campground and do hikes and different activities during the days and sleep in the same place each night. Adventurous people bike or paddle to a different campsite each night, while newer campers just camp in their backyards.

Car camping is a great way to see several different places in one trip.

Here are some basics about the different types of camping and places to camp. Later, we'll look at things you need for safe and comfortable camping no matter where you go.

Different Ways to Camp

The equipment you bring, how you set up your camp, and where you camp, depends on what type of camping you're doing. There are different kinds of camping, but let's just break them down into three types.

Car Camping: Basically, you park your car and camp nearby. During the day you might be hiking or fishing or riding bicycles, and in the evening you return to your camp. You might travel to a new campsite each day or stay at one campsite for a few days or a week, and before heading back home.

Many national parks are great places to go car camping. They offer spaces for both your car and your tent, plus have many activities to enjoy. You also get to meet other families who are in the same campground. Some national or state parks can get very busy, especially in the summer months. To make sure that your family has a spot at the park you want to visit, go to www.recreation.gov. This National Park Service site tells you how to find and reserve the right spot for your camping family.

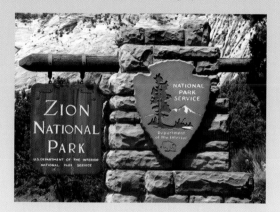

Backpacking: Maybe you've arrived at your campsite by walking there on a trail, carrying what you need in your backpack. Backpackers usually stay in one campsite for a number of nights and then walk back out. Another type of hiking plan might be to camp in a different site each night. You arrive in the late afternoon or evening, set up your camp, and then pack it all up the next morning and move on down the trail to another site.

Bicycle and Canoe/Kayak Camping: Packing your gear on a bike or a small boat is a bit different, but the equipment you need for a comfortable and safe night under the stars is pretty much the same as backpacking. The difference is that you carry it all on your bike or boat, plus you use that bike or boat to get from campsite to campsite.

With those last two types of camping, you're most likely going to be **self-sufficient**. That means you have to take care of yourself completely. You'll only have what you brought with you. There won't be any stores in the wilderness! When car camping, you can resupply regularly or shop for food. If you've forgotten something or broken a tent pole, for example, you can find a camping store for a replacement. When you're backpacking or on a bike, you have to learn to find your own solutions.

No matter what type of camping you choose, the goal is to have a safe and comfortable camping experience with adventures during the day, good food in the evening, songs and stories around the campfire, and a restful night's sleep under the stars.

Car Camping Basics

TEXT-DEPENDENT QUESTIONS

1. Name two basic types of camping.

2. What are two reasons the author cites for why people enjoy camping?

3. What is the main difference between backpacking and car camping?

RESEARCH PROJECT

Time to pick a campsite! Find out which national parks are near you and investigate their campsites. Do they allow car camping? Do they have campsites for backpackers? How many miles of trails can you find? What about rivers for canoeing? Explore and find a park near you that your family can visit.

CHAPTER 2

Getting It Done Right

t's late afternoon or getting near evening. The light is slanting from the west through the trees, and it's time to set up your campsite.

If you've arrived at your site by car, it's probably an established campground, so find your spot and get organized. You might have found a spot in a private campground, a local county campground, or even a state or national park.

 WORDS TO UNDERSTAND

doused put out, extinguished, usually with water and dirt

erosion the process by which the earth wears away or changes shape over time, affected by natural and man-made forces

rainfly an additional cover over the top of a tent to prevent rain from hitting the tent roof and possibly leaking in

You're on a backpacking trip, or bicycling or kayaking, and you've found a really nice site near a stream or river. After a long day of hiking, pedaling or paddling, it looks perfect! Before you relax, get to work setting up.

Here are some inside tips on creating a successful camp in either situation.

Car Camping Basics

Driving into the campground, you'll be assigned a campsite number and you'll pay a fee. Then you park the car where instructed (sometimes right next to your campsite). You've arrived! Breathe the fresh air, take a look around...and then get to work!

First priority: shelter. Most campgrounds will have a designated place for your tent. It's important to use this spot as it's probably well drained and won't puddle up if it rains. Also, using the designated site helps to control **erosion** and protects plant life by not having tents all over the place.

It's always a good idea to have your headlamp or flashlight nearby while you're putting your tent up. Darkness can sneak up on you while you're organizing camp, and it is really hard to find your headlamp in the dark.

Always organize your gear in the morning so you know where everything is in the evening. Put your headlamp/flashlight and your warm clothes in the same place every day. This is important for any type of camping . . . and it's a pretty good idea for life in general!

Before you go on your camping trip, set up your tent at home! This is really, really important. Make sure you have all the poles and stakes. Check that the **rainfly** and the main body of the tent are in good working condition, and that the zippers work. If it's a new tent, be sure to bring the directions. There are many different types of tents. Some of them are not so easy to set up the first time!

LEAVE NO TRACE

Cleaning up is as important as setting up. The idea is to leave your campsite with almost no trace that you were ever there. You should make a minimal impact on the campsite and the surrounding areas. This is called "Leave No Trace" camping. Here are some key things to keep in mind to camp this way.

■ Know Before You Go: Plan ahead so that you use marked trails and sites.

■ Choose The Right Path: Use those trails and campsites so you don't disturb animals and plants.

■ Trash Your Trash: Always pack out all your trash.

■ Leave What You Find: Don't bring home souvenirs of the wilderness; leave wild things, including plants, where they are.

■ Be Careful With Fire: Always make sure your campfires are completely doused.

■ Respect Wildlife: There are no tame wild animals; watch if you can, but leave them alone.

■ Be Kind To Other Visitors: Share your trails and respect others when in a campsite.

While someone is setting up the tent, another person could be arranging the kitchen. Get out the stove and fuel, the pots and pans, the food boxes.

If campfires are allowed, get the sticks and firewood stacked up and ready to go well before dark. (Note: Gathering firewood is not allowed in most car camps, so it's a good idea to bring your own, or see if the camp host has some available.)

Backpacking, Biking, and More

You might also arrive at camp after a day of hiking, pedaling your mountain bike, or paddling your canoe or kayak. Take a moment to slide off your pack and feel the pleasure of taking the weight off your shoulders and hips! Lean your bike against a tree or step out of your boat onto dry land. Stretch out as you take a look around your camp, your home for the night. You might be tired, but there is work to do.

It's always good to camp in a site that has been used before, a designated campsite with a fire pit. Many trail camps have a fire circle with a metal grate that you cook on. If you're lucky, someone who camped there before you left a pile of wood!

Be sure to go to the place in your pack where you put the stuff you'll need at the end of a hiking day: headlamp or flashlight and a warm layer of clothing. Even if it's been a warm day, odds are it will cool quickly in the evening as the sun nears the horizon. So put your jacket or sweater on, drink some water, and begin to settle in for the evening.

As with car camping, shelter is a priority, along with food and warmth. Put your tent up in a place where it looks like someone else before you put their tent. Check to see if the spot looks like it's ever had a puddle in it. Is a part of it lower than the surrounding area? Is there dried, cracked mud or dirt? If so, don't set up there because that's a place where water probably has collected at some point. You don't want water collecting under your tent during a nighttime rain shower. After trial and error, campers who came before you probably have found the best place. Clear out any sticks and stones, and take a look over your head, too. Don't set up under a damaged or loosely hanging tree branch.

Tents

There are so many different types of tents, and they all set up differently. Most have several parts in common, however. The bottom of the tent that is placed on the ground is called the footprint. The tent body is given structure by tent poles. Tent stakes hold the tent to the ground, and a rainfly made specifically for your tent covers the tent body and attaches with small ropes, clips, or Velcro. It's important to put the rainfly up properly. It keeps the tent dry! If you've done it right, it does not touch the main body of the tent, but sits a few inches above, keeping moisture out and even providing a layer of insulated air which can both warm and cool the inside of the tent.

First, slip the poles through the loops on the outside of the tent.

The flexible poles then anchor in small flaps at the corners of the tent.

Reminder: Set the tent up at least once at home before leaving on your trip. It can be a real challenge to figure out your tent for the first time in camp after a long day, possibly even in the dark!

As you take each part of the tent out of its bag, make a plan for keeping track of the bags. Best bet is to put all the bags into one bag and tie that to one of the tent ropes so it can't blow away.

Then, unroll your sleeping pad and sleeping bag and lay them out inside the tent. Fluff the sleeping bag out so it can be all snug and puffy and warm when you're ready for sleep in your cozy shelter.

Zip the tent doors closed on your way out. That helps keep out bugs and creatures and keeps the tent warmer when you want to sleep in it later on.

No matter how you arrive at your campsite, preparing your sleeping place should be your top priority. Learning the right way to set up a tent will make your camping adventure a comfortable one.

TEXT-DEPENDENT QUESTIONS

1. What does "Leave No Trace" mean?

2. Why are rainflys important?

3. When looking for a place to put your tent, why should you look up?

RESEARCH PROJECT

Do you own a tent? If so, go set it up in the backyard. See if you have all the parts you need...and how fast you can set it up! If you don't own a tent, go online and examine the different types. Tents come in many sizes, usually based on how many people they can fit. What sort of tent do you think would work for you?

Setting Up a Tent

CHAPTER 3

Get Great Gear

he weather and the seasons determine what type of gear you're going to need. Outside, it could be hot and dry, or cold and rainy, or anything else in between. You need to make sure that the gear you bring is right for the season, right for the place you're going, and right for the type of camping you'll do.

Car Camping Gear

he advantage of car camping is being able to take a bit more gear than if you're just backpacking.

 WORDS TO UNDERSTAND

biodegradable able to be broken down into natural ingredients

miso a type of Japanese soup made from fish stock

perishable describing food that will go bad over time or without refrigeration

Along with the backpacking list on page 30—plus all the gear you need for your tent and shelter—here are a few ideas to make your car camping adventure a winner.

The best bet is to organize the gear into categories, and load each category into sealable plastic boxes with the name of the category written on top. For instance, a food/pantry box (or two or three), kitchen items box, nighttime camp items box(es) for tents and sleeping bags, etc., and either a box or duffle bag for each person's clothing and personal items.

Then, you can just slide the boxes in the car or truck and you're ready to go! It sure makes it easier to set up your new camp in the evening. A good idea to keep in mind is that your camping spot is really a simple version of your home: the tent is the bedroom, the picnic bench and campfire are the kitchen. (And the stars are your roof!)

A camp kitchen setup includes many of these items, just like home!

As you unpack, take the boxes with your cooking and kitchen supplies and put them next to the picnic table. In one box you've got a really simplified version of your kitchen at home: cooking pots, bowls, knife/fork/spoons, etc. In another, you have non-**perishable** food items. You could say you've got everything but the kitchen sink, but this is car camping, so bring a small plastic tub as a sink, with some soap and a scrubber. Set up a washing area away from the table.

In your ice chest you've got the perishable food items and maybe some cold drinks. Set your stove up carefully on the table, making sure it's stable and level. Put a garbage bag near your cooking area, and see how neat you can keep your camp. And, if you're camping well, see how little trash you have. Put this in an animal-proof place at night, too!

Note: After dinner, be sure to put the ice chest and all food items in a safe place away from animals. Many campgrounds have locking food boxes for each campsite. Use it! Or, put all food items, ice chest, etc., back in the car and make sure the windows are rolled all the way up.

Put the first aid kit where it can be located easily, and let everyone know where it is. Set up your lantern and get your headlamps/flashlights ready before dark. After you're finished eating, take some time to clean up and organize, put stuff away, and then get out the evening's entertainment. Musical instruments are essential to any time around a campfire. Camping musicians might bring guitars, ukeleles, fiddles, and a few songbooks with chords and words. A campfire without music is like stars without twinkles.

Backpacking Gear

Now, let's take a good look at backpacking equipment. It's way different than car camping! The goal is simplicity. You and your friends will be carrying everything you need. Let's think about that for a second. How about remembering this: if you're carrying everything you need, *you should need everything you are carrying!*

Experienced backpacker campers have their favorite gear list. Some like to go super lightweight, and they bring only essential items. Others

Backpacking Gear

prefer to have some of the comforts of home, and choose to carry some extra pounds. And some, usually less-experienced backpackers, try to re-create most of the comforts of home and bring way too much, which can make the backpacking experience not very much fun.

It's best to organize your simplified packing list around essential items in various categories. Here's a list of recommended backpacking gear:

- Backpack: lightweight internal frame
- Sleeping bag and pad
- Shelter: tent or tarp
- Raingear: pants and jacket and/or poncho
- Stove and fuel
- Waterproof matches
- Cookpot and fork/spoon/knife
- Water bottles
- First aid kit
- Emergency blanket: made from foil and carried in your first aid kit
- Garbage bags
- Whistle and mirror: for emergency
- Map, compass, GPS
- Pencil and paper
- Headlamp and batteries
- Sunscreen, lip protection, bug repellent
- Hiking pole(s)
- Sunglasses
- **Biodegradable** toilet paper, small trowel
- Lightweight small nylon cord, about 25 feet
- Fix-it kit: rubber bands, duct tape wrapped around your water bottle; safety pins; needle and thread (dental floss works well!)
- Personal hygiene: toothbrush and toothpaste, small bar of biodegradable soap, small PakTowel

Clothing: Think Layering!

No matter where or how you go camping, you need to dress for success. And in the case of camping and living outdoors, success means having clothing that has a function. We humans need to keep our body temperatures somewhere in the "Goldilocks Zone." That's right—not too hot, not too cold.

Here's an example. Let's start with our head—a hat for shade during the day, a wool beanie at night. Keep the sun off during the day, and keep the heat in during the night.

Layers are important. Rather than one big jacket for when it's cold, and one small thin shirt for when it's hot, think layers. The temperature outside is always changing through the day, as is our own body temperature. You should have a nice light synthetic undershirt, perhaps a fleece or flannel shirt over that, and then a down-filled or synthetic puffy jacket. And, of course, a waterproof rain jacket. You can take these on or off as needed during the day and into the evening. Not too hot, not too cold.

Socks should be layered too, to protect your feet from blisters as you hike and go on adventures during the day. A pair of lightweight silk liner socks with wool socks over the liners is a great combo. And bring some heavier wool socks for when you're snug in your sleeping bag at night. Keeping your head and feet warm is important, and sure feels nice! Wool gloves are important, too, for when it gets really cold. Keep them in your jacket pocket.

Think layers for your legs, too. Wear long pants, and put on a pair

Long sleeves can be worn over a T-shirt; pants can zip into shorts.

of long underwear under your pants for warmth in the evening. You might try a pair of rugged shorts for during the day, but keep a good pair of waterproof rain pants handy just in case.

Camp Food

ood tastes so delicious when you're taking a break on the trail, sitting at sunset in your camp, or readying yourself at dawn for another day of adventure. There are a few requirements that you should keep in mind. All the food you bring has to be nutritious, lightweight, and compact. It needs to be easily prepared, and it can't need refrigeration or ice.

There are many good websites on food for camping backpackers. Here's an overview of possibilities:

Breakfast:

Cereal (granola or instant oatmeal with dried fruit and berries and powdered milk), hot cocoa.

Lunch:

Often on the trail, lunch is eaten several times during the day while taking hiking breaks. Beef jerky or salami, dried fruit, nuts, chocolate, peanut butter, tortillas or pita bread. Whole grain crackers, cheese that doesn't need refrigeration, energy bars.

Dinner:

A cup of soup or **miso** as a first course. Prepared dehydrated meals, pasta, rice, couscous. Tsampa soup (which is roasted whole grains and vegetables traditionally eaten by Tibetans for energy at high altitudes), dried meat or fish. Cocoa, chocolate.

There are a couple of different ways to organize and pack your food. You can pack it in meal categories. Make one bag for breakfast stuff, one for lunch, one for dinner. Another way is to organize it into daily meals. A breakfast, a lunch, and a dinner, each in their own Ziplock bags, and then the three bags put inside a larger Ziplock bag. Label the bag "Day 2," or "Wednesday," and you'll be super organized.

HOW TO CHOOSE THE RIGHT SHOES

If your feet are unhappy, the rest of your body will be too. So you want to have shoes that are comfortable and rugged for around camp and on your adventures. Shoes should give support and traction. Trail technology for our feet has come a long way, so you won't need a pair of big, heavy boots to be safe and functional outdoors. You can use trail-running or low-top hiking shoes—Vibram or "lug soled" shoes are the best bet. These are durable and have great traction.

Shoes also come with or without water-resistant "Gore-Tex" construction. You have to think about what your use is going to be. Gore-Tex keeps most of the water out if you're hiking in moist conditions, which can be good. Lighter non-Gore-Tex shoes breathe much better and your feet don't get as sweaty (and maybe stinky). However, if you do get water in while crossing a creek, the water stays in with Gore-Tex, but flows easily out with non-Gore-Tex.

Sizing is very important! You'll be wearing two layers of socks, so you want to try on the shoes with those same socks on your feet. You don't want the shoes too tight, as you'll get blisters for sure. But not too loose, either, as you don't want your feet to slip around in the shoes . . . and you definitely don't want them to slide off while you're walking!

Choose the Right Shoes

CAR CAMPING FOOD

Because of the added space you have for bringing food, the possibilities are endless for car camping! Burgers, hot dogs, spaghetti, and more. It all tastes so good when you're outside. Bring the basics with you in the car, plus you can shop at stores for perishable items as you go. Here's a list of items you may want to have in your portable pantry:

Cocoa/hot chocolate
Cereal
Bread, jam, peanut butter, and honey
Pancake mix, syrup
Eggs
Milk (fresh or powdered)
Salt and pepper, herbs and spices
Crackers and cheese
Dried soup mixes
Beef jerky
Energy bars
Granola and nuts, or trail mix (pictured)
Dried fruit and vegetables
Powdered drink mixes
Marshmallows, chocolate bars, graham crackers

TEXT-DEPENDENT QUESTIONS

1. How should you arrange your gear for car camping?

2. What phrase does the author use to help you pack for a backpacking trip?

3. Name one thing the author suggests as a good trail lunch food.

 ## RESEARCH PROJECT

Menu time! Pretend that you're going out with friends for a three-day backpacking trip. You'll have to carry and cook all your own food. Make a schedule of what food you'll have at each meal of the trip. What ingredients do you need? Are you getting the right nutrition? What snacks will you bring?

CHAPTER 4

Further Adventures

With the basics of food and shelter taken care of and your plans for the day set, what about nighttime? Ahh, yes, the campfire. The center of your camp, the place to gather around, to tell stories, to heat water and to cook your dinner if you're not using a stove. For as long as humans have been humans we've gathered around the fire with friends and community. Maybe it's what makes us human, harnessing the power of wood to stay warm, to cook food, and to bring a circle of light

WORDS TO UNDERSTAND

dehydrated food that has had most of the water removed and/or has been freeze-dried

propane a popular type of gas fuel used in small devices such as stoves and lanterns

tinder small, dry pieces of material used to ignite a larger fire

into the dark night. Sitting around the fire at night under the stars with your friends, telling stories and sharing laughter, listening to the nighttime quiet with just the crackling of burning wood and the glow of embers is the best thing ever!

Of course, fire can be dangerous, too, and experienced campers know how to be fire-smart and fire-safe. Care of the fire and fire prevention are the responsibilities of a camper. It's as important to know how to put a fire out as it is how to light and maintain your fire.

A ring of rocks makes for a safe campfire site.

A good campfire is:
1. built in a safe place that helps to control it
2. just large enough to serve your needs using the least amount of wood
3. kept under control and watched at all times
4. put OUT when no longer needed

Picking the Spot

lways use an established fire ring or fire pit for your campfire. This will be easy to spot in your campsite, as it will almost always be a circle or rectangle of stones with ash or coals from previous fires. It might be a three-sided metal box with a grate over the top. If you're lucky, when you arrive at your campsite you might find that some other camper had left behind a nice stack of wood for you. That is a great thing for you to do when you're leaving the site—pass it on!

Never have your fire under or near a tree or bush. Clear the area around the fire pit of all leaves, dried grass, and sticks down to the dirt. Keep a shovel or small trowel by the fire at all times, as well as a few bottles or buckets of water. Most wilderness areas require a campfire permit, which you need to get at a ranger station or forest headquarters before you start your camping adventure.

Fuel and How to Use It

ather the fuel you'll need before lighting the fire. There are three types of material you'll need for your fire. Make a separate stack of each.

Tinder: the stuff that catches fire from a match. Tinder can be little shavings from dry sticks, small sticks thinner than a pencil, the fuzz from some trees' dry split bark. Inexperienced campers often try to light a bunch of dry grass or leaves, which flare up quickly, make smoke and then burn out, with not enough heat to get the fire going. Tinder

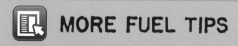
Wood for kindling should *snap!* when broken; sticks that bend are too green and won't burn well.

Wood that crumbles is rotten. Its energy is pretty well gone. It will smoke and not burn well and won't give off much heat.

Try to use wood that isn't lying on the ground, or hasn't been there too long. Ground wood can be too damp for good burning.

Bonus tip for tinder: before you leave home, take some cotton balls, cover them with Vaseline and put them in a Ziplock bag. Use one each time you need to start your fire. Lay your tinder gently over it, and light the cotton ball, which will burn for a few minutes while you add fuel. (These work great in wet weather!)

Build the fire using light tinder and small kindling sticks.

should be really small and very dry. Most any little twigs will do, ranging in size from matchstick to pencil thickness. Make a stack right near the fire circle, so you can feed the fire as it grows. (Paper can be used, of course, but it's a nice skill to see if you can start your fire without it.) As you face the fire and light it, the breeze should be at your back. This will make a draft that blows through the fire and gets it going.

Kindling: Dry sticks and twigs, ranging in size from pieces pencil thin up to a thumb's thickness. Each piece should be around six to twelve inches in length. Add the pieces gently in an A-shape over the burning tinder.

Fuel: this is the real fire material that keeps your fire going. Use good, firm and dry pieces of wood, ranging in size from just thicker than kindling up to arm's thickness, or thicker, depending on the use of your fire, and how long you want it to burn. (A note for busy campgrounds: wood gathering is not permitted in most larger parks. Check the regulations on the National Forest Service website for your area.)

Once your fire is going well, you'll need to let the fire burn to make coals. Those are the best when using your fire to cook or heat water. Put the fire grate down over the glowing coals, carefully put your covered pot on the grate, and you're ready to move toward dinner!

Camp Stoves

Some places do not allow or have safe places for campfires. That's no problem for an experienced camper. A variety of small, portable camp stoves can be used for cooking (though they're not quite as much fun as a campfire, of course!).

When car camping, you'll probably want to use a two-burner **propane** stove. These are generally known as "Coleman stoves," from the camping supply company that popularized them in the 1950s. Make sure your stove is level and steady, follow the directions for attaching the fuel supply, and you're ready to cook.

Backpacking stoves are used by just about everyone who is carrying all their gear. They are lightweight, fuel-efficient, and there are many,

A campstove makes heating water for tea or coffee easy.

many different types. To begin with, you'll have to ask yourself a few questions:

What type of cooking are you doing? Boiling water as quickly and as efficiently as possible, or simmering your dinner slowly for a longer period of time? How many people are in your group? How long will you be out on the trail?

The two main types are canister stoves and liquid fuel stoves. Also available are alternative fuel stoves and wood-burning twig stoves.

Canister Stoves: These are super efficient and burn very hot, bringing water to a boil quickly. (If you're planning on preparing **dehydrated** [freeze-dried], pre-packaged meals, you just add boiling water and you're ready to go!) These types of stoves require fuel canisters of pre-pressurized gases: usually isobutane and propane. Isobutane burns hot and clean, even in cold temperatures. The canister self seals when the stove is detached, so you can't spill any and it won't leak in your pack. However, the canisters have to be thrown out after they're empty, and when you're cooking you can't tell how much fuel you have remaining. They tend to not burn as hot when the fuel canister is getting low. Most canister stoves burn with a hot flame and are made to boil water quickly.

The actual fuel canisters usually hold eight ounces, which should boil about 30 pints of water (about 60 cups). A freeze-dried meal for two needs about three cups of water to rehydrate, so do the math: a canister might be good for about 15 to 20 meals. (Tip: If it's windy or really cold, the stove won't be quite as efficient.)

Liquid Fuel Stoves: These stoves run on liquid white gas, or naphtha. They burn hot and clean, and do well in below-freezing temperatures. Compared to the per-ounce price of canister fuel, they are much less costly. You can buy the fuel in larger containers and fill up the fuel bottles before your trip. You can tell how much fuel you have remaining and the flame stays hot even when the fuel is low. Most liquid fuel stoves can be set to simmer, for some slow-cooking gourmet meals. Downside of these stoves? The fuel is liquid, so you have to be careful of spills or leaks in your pack. Also, lighting them is a little trickier, and following the directions for priming the stove when lighting takes a little practice. Hint: As with setting up a tent, practice at home! With the stove and fuel bottle, it may weigh a bit more than a canister stove, but you aren't having to carry back and then wastefully throw-out an empty fuel canister, sending it to a landfill or hazardous waste site.

Alternative Fuel Stoves: These are efficient for cooking and boiling water, although a little more slowly. Denatured alcohol stoves weigh very little and burn quietly, as they do not use pressurized fuel. You'll be carrying a separate container of liquid fuel, so there's still the challenge of not spilling or leaking.

Solid-fuel tablet stoves are useful for backpackers who want very little weight and bulk. They are super-light, small, and inexpensive. Also, there's no worry about liquid fuel; the fuel comes in little pellets or cubes. They burn more slowly than the other liquid and canister fuels.

Wood-burning backpacking stoves use small twigs and sticks as fuel. They are usually about the size of a water bottle and are quite efficient. They are an environmentally sound choice in terms of fuel, and you burn

The best part of camping? The time around the campfire with family and friends.

what you find. Then again, they can't be used where wood gathering is prohibited. They are much less expensive to purchase and operate, and give off the warmth and glow of a mini-campfire while cooking. They are easy to use for simmering, as you're the one feeding the mini-twigs and sticks into it.

As the fire dies down in the evening and you get ready to sleep, you can lie under the stars or in your tent knowing that you've had a great day. You planned ahead, brought what you needed, and successfully made your "home" in the outdoors. You'll wake with the sun, clean up, leave no trace, and head out for your next adventure. Who knows what you'll find?

 ## TEXT-DEPENDENT QUESTIONS

1. What should a fire be at all times?
2. What is tinder and how is it used?
3. Name two kinds of stoves the author describes.

 ## RESEARCH PROJECT

Look up information about the stoves the author mentions. Write up a short report on why you'd choose one kind over another. Remember to think about what type of camping you might do or what kind of food you might be cooking.

FIND OUT MORE

WEBSITES

www.thecampingfamily.com/camping-menu-ideas.html
Great ideas for meal planning for family camping.

lnt.org
The Leave No Trace organization has ideas for you to keep your campsite nature-friendly.

www.forestcamping.com/dow/list/nflist.htm
Find a campground in a National Forest on this site.

www.nps.gov/index.htm
The National Park Service site has lots of ideas for parks and campgrounds to explore all around the country.

BOOKS

Brunelle, Lynn. *Camp Out! The Ultimate Kids' Guide.* New York: Workman Publishing, 2007.
Fun illustrations make reading this step-by-step guide to camping out almost as fun as . . . camping!

Fletcher, Colin. *The Thousand Mile Summer.* Berkeley, Calif.: Howell-North Books, 1964.
This is the author's chronicle of his 1958 hike along the entire eastern edge of California. Fletcher writes of traveling on foot along the Colorado River, though Death Valley and the High Sierra.

George, Jean Craighead. *My Side of the Mountain* (Puffin Modern Classics). New York: Puffin Books, 2004.
This is a well-known and beloved novel with great camping sections—very inspirational and practical.

bushcraft wilderness skills, named for the remote bush country of Australia

camouflage a pattern or disguise in clothing designed to make it blend in to the surroundings

conservation the act of preserving or protecting, such as an environment or species

ecosystem the habitats of species and the ways that species interact with each other

friction the resistance that happens when two surfaces rub together

insulation protection from something, such as extreme hot or cold

layering adding layers of clothing to stay warm and removing layers to cool off.

rewilding returning to a more natural state

synthetic manmade, often to imitate a natural material

traction the grip or contact that an object has with another surface

wake the waves produced by the movement of a boat

INDEX

PHOTO CREDITS

ABOUT THE AUTHOR

Jim Brady has been a teacher and outdoor trip leader all of his adult life. He's led cultural and camping adventures with young people for the past 40 years in Bolivia, Australia, England, Hawaii, Baja California, Kenya, and all across the USA. He and his wife taught in Kenya for the US Peace Corps in the 1970s and for a US State Department Refugee Training program in Thailand in the 1980s. He's currently teaching Human Geography at Santa Barbara Middle School and serves as Assistant Head of School and Dean of Students. He also helps lead at least four trips each year, from bicycling to backpacking to mule packing into the local Los Padres Wilderness. Jim lives on a cattle ranch, enjoys surfing, biking and playing music, and likes nothing more than to take a hike every night and look up to see the sky.